Backyard Bloodsuckers

Questions, Facts & Tongue Twisters About Creepy, Crawly Creatures

Mike Artell

Good Year Books

An Imprint of Pearson Learning

Photo credits:

Front cover: *t.* ©USDA/Science Source/Photo Researchers, Inc.; *m.* E.R. Degginger/Color-Pic, Inc.; *b.* James H. Robinson/Animals Animals. Back cover: Jack Clark/Animals Animals. Title page: *t.*©USDA/Science Source/Photo Researchers, Inc.; *m.* E.R. Degginger/Color-Pic, Inc. 3: ©Dr. Tony Brain/Science Photo Library/Photo Researchers, Inc. 8: Jack Clark/Animals Animals. 9: Hans Pfletschinger/Peter Arnold, Inc. 10: C. James Webb/Phototake. 13: ©USDA/Science Source/Photo Researchers, Inc. 14: ©Dr. Tony Brain/Science Photo Library/Photo Researchers, Inc. 18: *t.* David Scharf/Peter Arnold, Inc.; *b.* ©Syd Greenberg/Photo Researchers, Inc. 21: Dwight R. Kuhn. 22: ©Stephen Dalton/Photo Researchers, Inc. 23: ©Gary Retherford/Photo Researchers, Inc. 26: James H. Robinson/Animals Animals. 27: Raymond C. Mendez/Animals Animals. 28: E.R. Degginger/Color-Pic, Inc. 29: ©Noble Proctor/Photo Researchers, Inc. 31: Jane Burton/Bruce Coleman, Inc. 32: ©Ken Eward/Photo Researchers, Inc. 36: ©Oliver Meckes/Photo Researchers, Inc. 39: Tim Flach/Tony Stone Images. 41: David Scharf/Peter Arnold, Inc. 44: *t., m.* Arthur M. Siegelman/Visuals Unlimited; *b.* Ken Lucas/Visuals Unlimited. 46: David Scharf/Peter Arnold, Inc. 47: Bill Beatty/Visuals Unlimited. 48: David Scharf/Peter Arnold, Inc. 53: S.J. Krasemann/Peter Arnold, Inc. 55: ©Martin Dohrn/Photo Researchers, Inc. 57: ©Meckes/Ottawa/Photo Researchers, Inc. 60: ©Gregory G. Dimijian/Photo Researchers, Inc. 63: James H. Robinson/Animals Animals. 64: J. Paling/Animals Animals. 65: C. Milkins/Animals Animals. 67: ©Oliver Meckes/Photo Researchers, Inc. 71: Al Lamme/Phototake. 72: ©Rondi/Tani/Photo Researchers, Inc. 75: ©USDA/Science Source/Photo Researchers, Inc. 76: *t.*Dwight R. Kuhn; *b.*E.R. Degginger/Color-Pic, Inc. 77: David Scharf/Peter Arnold, Inc. 78: *t.* S.J. Krasemann/Peter Arnold, Inc.; *b.* James H. Robinson/Animals Animals.

62: Courtesy of The Pearson Museum, Southern Illinois University School of Medicine.

 Good Year Books

are available for most basic curriculum subjects plus many enrichment areas. For more Good Year Books, contact your local bookseller or educational dealer. For a complete catalog with information about other Good Year Books, please write:

Good Year Books
299 Jefferson Road
Parsippany, NJ 07054

Book design by Sean O'Neill, Christine Ronan Design.
Design Manager: M. Jane Heelan
Editor: Roberta Dempsey
Editorial Manager: Suzanne Beason
Executive Editor: Judith Adams

PREFACE

Most of the creatures described in this book are arthropods. Arthropods are creatures that have legs with joints and skeletons on the outside of their bodies. Some of the arthropods you'll meet in this book are mosquitoes, fleas, and ticks. You may think there are a lot of humans on Earth, but there are a lot more arthropods. In fact, approximately 80 percent of all the creatures in the animal kingdom are arthropods.

Other bloodsucking creatures in this book (such as leeches) are not arthropods. They're actually weird worms. The amazing thing about all of these creatures is that they feed on human and animal blood.

You're probably wondering why these backyard bloodsuckers want our blood. Why don't these creatures just eat other, smaller creatures, or plants? The reason is that bloodsucking creatures don't have all the chemicals in their bodies that they need to reproduce. They have to get those chemicals from human or animal blood. And since our blood is inside of us, bloodsuckers need to penetrate our skin to get to it. That means they have to bite us.

Human blood is made up of four basic ingredients: plasma, red blood cells, white blood cells, and platelets. Plasma is a light yellow liquid. Plasma contains water, salt, and the proteins that bloodsucking animals need to reproduce.

Red blood cells are oxygen carriers. When you breathe, your lungs transfer the oxygen to the red blood cells, which deliver the oxygen to the rest of your body.

White blood cells are your body's "soldiers." They attack bacteria, viruses, and anything else that might be harmful to your body.

Platelets help you to stop bleeding if you get cut. They make your blood clot.

The blood cells in your body are very, very small. There are approximately 25 billion red blood cells, 35 million white blood cells, and 1.5 billion platelets in a single teaspoon of blood. You've probably seen a two-liter plastic soda bottle. If you drained the average human body of all of its blood, it would fill about two of those two-liter bottles. For more information about human blood, check out these Web sites:

http://www.micscape.simplenet.com/mag/articles/blood1.html
http://www.ktca.org/newtons/10/bloodtype.html
http://www.pa.msu.edu/~sciencet/ask_st/061197.html

About the Author

Mike Artell has written and illustrated more than 30 books and has hosted his own television cartooning show. Mike likes to write and illustrate nonfiction books because he learns so much while doing the research for them. Mike also likes to write and illustrate joke books, riddle books, and tongue twister books because they make him laugh while he's writing them. Mike lives near New Orleans, Louisiana. He's married to Susan, a high school science teacher. They have two daughters (Stephanie and Joanna), a cat (Simba), a rabbit (Smokey), and two fish (Pisces and Aquarius).

TABLE of CONTENTS

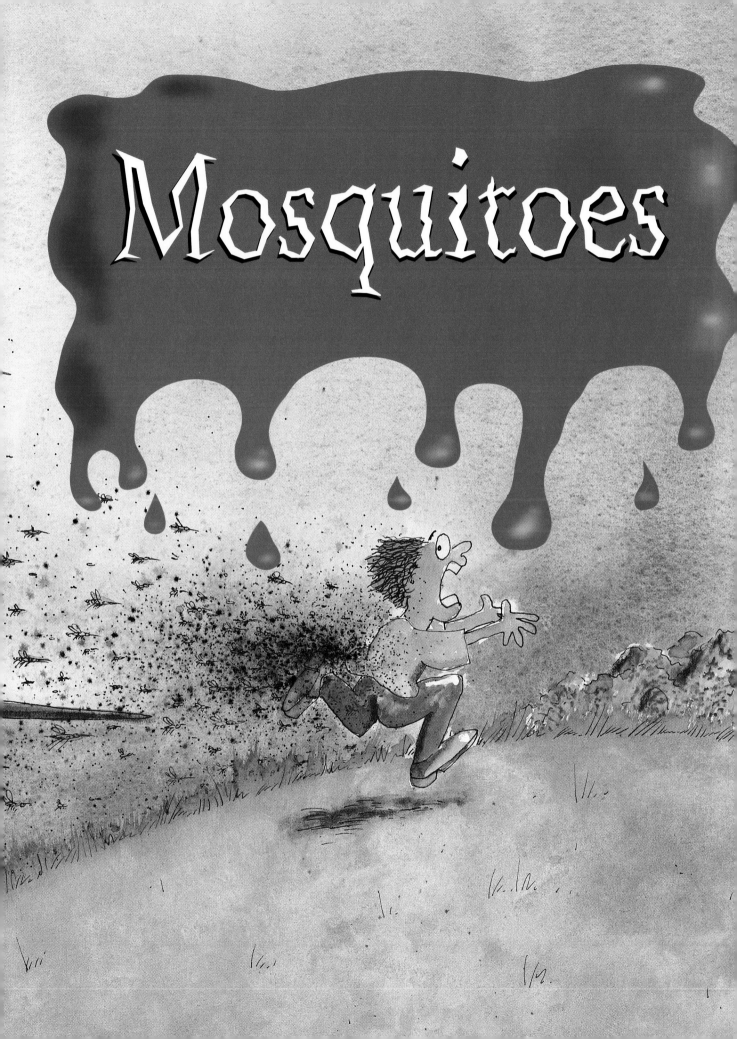

Mosquitoes

Bzzz... Bzzz....

Mosquitoes might be the most annoying insects on Earth. When they're not sticking you with their pointy little mouths and sucking your blood, they're buzzing around your ears while you're trying to sleep.

Backyard Bloodsuckers Bulletin

YO SOY... EL MUSKETA!

The word *mosquitoes* comes from the Spanish word *musketas*, which means, "little flies." That's a very good name for them, because mosquitoes are actually a type of fly.

What Do They **EAT?**

Is blood the only thing that mosquitoes drink? Nope. In fact, male mosquitoes never drink blood—they drink nectar from plants and flowers. Only female mosquitoes drink blood. Females usually drink nectar too, but when they are ready to reproduce, they need some of the chemicals that are contained in blood in order to produce eggs. So the next time you get a mosquito bite, you'll know that it was a girl mosquito that bit you.

Mosquitoes don't live very long. Some species live as long as 5 or 6 months, but most usually only live about 14 days. That doesn't count the ones that get eaten by animals or squished by people.

Why don't you see many mosquitoes during the winter? Do they hibernate? Mosquitoes don't go into a state of true hibernation, but their bodies do slow down a lot during the winter.

During their lifetimes, mosquitoes go through four separate stages. The first stage is the egg stage. Most mosquitoes lay their eggs on the surface of standing water, although some lay their eggs in damp soil and then wait for the soil to become flooded. The eggs are stuck together and form a little "raft," which floats on the surface of the water. In a day or so, the eggs hatch and mosquito larvae appears. This is the beginning of the second stage of the mosquito's life.

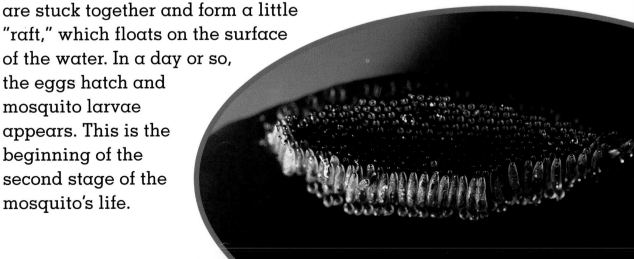

Mosquito LARVA

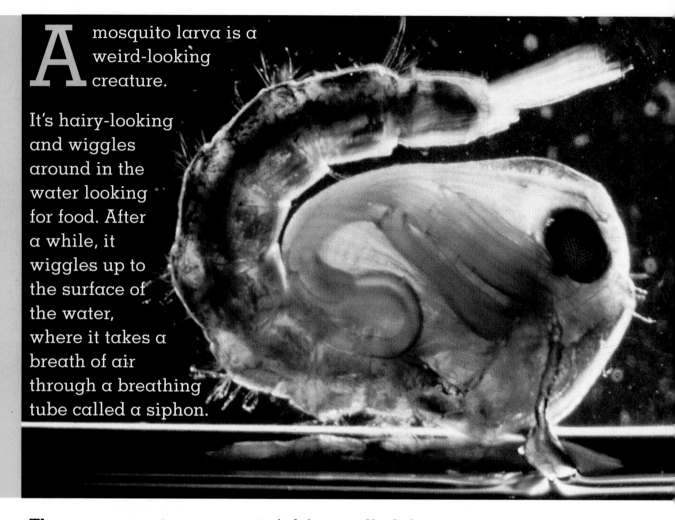

A mosquito larva is a weird-looking creature.

It's hairy-looking and wiggles around in the water looking for food. After a while, it wiggles up to the surface of the water, where it takes a breath of air through a breathing tube called a siphon.

The next stage in a mosquito's life is called the pupa stage. During this stage, mosquitoes begin to change. They stop eating and develop two breathing tubes called trumpets. They also change shape and develop a pupal case. It is in this case that they change into an adult mosquito.

VERY COOL.

When the mosquito has changed into a fully formed adult, it splits out of the pupal case and stands on the surface of the water so its body can harden.

That's when the trouble starts.

Backyard Bloodsuckers
Bulletin

If it's warm enough and conditions are right, it's possible for some species of mosquitoes to go from the egg stage to the adult stage in about 4 days.

How Do I Keep Them AWAY?

How can we control the mosquito population? The best way to control the number of mosquitoes in your area is to eliminate the mosquitoes' favorite breeding places. As you read earlier, mosquitoes' eggs, larvae, and pupae need water to grow. Almost any place outside that you find containers of water, you'll find mosquito eggs, larvae, and pupae. Here are some of the favorite places mosquitoes pick to lay their eggs:

- old tires

- birdbaths

- rain gutters

- wading pools

- barbeque grills

- water-filled tree holes

- pans under potted plants

- pet dishes

It's important to clean up these mosquito breeding grounds if you want to cut down on the mosquito population.

A wet, grassy area about the size of a page in this book can produce 1,000 mosquito larvae.

Another way to get rid of mosquitoes is to encourage mosquito predators, such as bats and dragonflies. Although you may think of bats as bloodsuckers too, not all bats drink blood. In fact, many species of bats are insect eaters. Did you know that one hungry bat can eat 600 mosquitoes in an hour?

You can also reduce the number of mosquitoes near you by adding turtles or mosquito-eating minnows to pools of water. Some minnows just love to eat mosquito eggs, larvae, and pupae.

Of course, another great way to get rid of mosquitoes is to wait until one lands on your skin, and then . . .

Backyard Bloodsuckers
Bulletin

Most mosquitoes keep their bodies horizontal when they bite, but the Anopheles mosquito sticks its rear end up in the air when it bites.

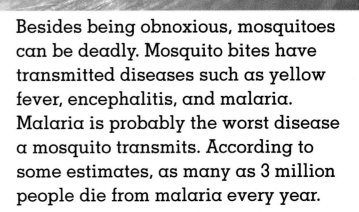

Besides being obnoxious, mosquitoes can be deadly. Mosquito bites have transmitted diseases such as yellow fever, encephalitis, and malaria. Malaria is probably the worst disease a mosquito transmits. According to some estimates, as many as 3 million people die from malaria every year.

MORE on **Mosquitoes**

- Most mosquitoes only live a couple of weeks.

- Only female mosquitoes bite.

- Mosquitoes go through four stages in their lives: egg, larva, pupa, and adult.

- Old tires and other containers are breeding grounds for mosquitoes.

- Mosquitoes can carry deadly diseases.

- A mosquito's wings flap 300 to 400 times each second.

- More than 2,700 species of mosquitoes have been identified.

Do You Want to Know MORE?

Log on to these Web sites to learn more about mosquitoes:

- http://www.mosquito.org/mosquito.html

- http://www.mosquitoes.net/

- http://www.ent.iastate.edu/imagegal/diptera/culicidae/

- http://martin.parasitology.mcgill.ca/JIMSPAGE/PLASMOD.HTM

- http://whyfiles.news.wisc.edu/071questions/7.html

- http://www-rci.rutgers.edu/~insects/njmos.htm

- http://www.gurnee.il.us/public_works/mosquitoes.html

- http://whyfiles.news.wisc.edu/016skeeter/index.html

- http://www.ag.ohio-state.edu/~ohioline/hyg-fact/2000/2148.html

- http://fiona.umsmed.edu/~yar/arbo.html

Also, look in your local phone book to see if your state or county has a "mosquito abatement" organization. Often, these people visit schools and talk about the ways you can reduce the number of mosquitoes where you live.

WHOA!

TIC TIC..

YUK!

Can you imagine a nastier creature than a flea? There are lots of different kinds of fleas. There are dog fleas and cat fleas and rabbit fleas and rat fleas, but all of them are a bother to humans and their pets. Like mosquitoes, fleas go through four life-cycle stages: egg, larva, pupa, and adult. Flea eggs are smooth and white. Eggs may take anywhere from two days to two weeks to hatch into larvae.

The larvae look like little hairy worms. They're about 1/4 inch long and have brown heads and yellowish bodies. Although the larvae are blind, they prefer dark places where they can hide.

I'M NOT COMING OUT OF THIS EGG UNTIL SOMEBODY TURNS THAT LIGHT OFF!

Backyard Bloodsuckers Bulletin

One way to tell if your house has fleas is to place a plate with a little water and some dishwashing detergent on the floor. If you place a lamp with a long neck over the plate,

What Do They EAT?

I THINK I'M GOING TO BE SICK...

The larvae have a most disgusting diet. They do not suck blood, but instead eat dead skin, hair, digested blood from the adult fleas' feces, and other nauseating stuff.

After a while, each larva spins a little silken cocoon around itself and becomes a pupa. Most of the time, the pupa remains in its cocoon for a week or two. But if there is no food source around (such as an animal or human being), the pupa may stay in its cocoon for months.

the adult fleas will be attracted to the light from the lamp. When they jump toward the light, some of them will fall back into the plate. The dishwashing detergent makes it hard for the fleas to stay on the surface of the water and they drown. If you find dead fleas in the plate, your house has fleas.

When the pupa detects movement or carbon dioxide from a living creature's breath, it will emerge from the cocoon as an adult flea. And after all that time in its cocoon, it is very hungry! Once the young adult fleas emerge from their cocoons, they need to drink some blood within a few days or they'll die.

BLOOD! MUST HAVE BLOOD...

How Do I Keep Them AWAY?

If there are fleas in your house, chances are only about 5 percent of them are biting adults. Usually, about half of the population are eggs, 30 percent are larvae and about 15 percent are pupae.

I'M NOT A FIGHTER... I'M A LARVA!

THAT TICKLES!

Do you know why it's hard to squish a flea? Fleas are small and have hard bodies. Human fingers are soft on the ends. Fleas are just too hard and your fingers are too soft. What makes squishing a flea even harder is the shape of the flea's body. It's flattened vertically, sort of like a fish. Fleas are shaped this way so they can move through animal and human hair easily. When you squeeze it, the flea's body just gets a little skinnier.

Tongue Twister

Try saying this tongue twister three times fast: **Freddie found fifty filthy fleas in Fido's fur.**

The best way to control fleas is to make sure your pets are free of them. Check pet areas regularly and vacuum around the places where they sleep and lie.

How Do They MOVE?

When it comes to jumping, fleas are hard to beat. A typical flea can jump as high as 7 inches and as far as 13 inches.

If that doesn't seem like a lot to you, think about this: if you could jump as high and as far as a flea, you could jump 250 feet in the air and 450 feet down the street.

WOO HOO!

DID YOU SEE THAT?

Fleas have made a lot of people and animals sick. Because fleas jump around a lot, they often bite one animal or person, then jump to another animal or person and bite them. In doing this, they can spread lots of diseases. In the fourteenth century, fleas spread a disease in Europe called "the plague" or "Black Death," and millions of people died. Fleas are also known to spread typhus and tapeworms in animals.

WHEN Will I See Them?

Fleas like warm weather. That's why you see them most often in the summer. They like temperatures between 70 and 85 degrees Fahrenheit. They also like humid weather. When the humidity is around 70 percent, fleas are the happiest.

Sometimes people talk about "sand fleas," but there's really no such thing. Sand and gravel are excellent breeding places for fleas, so they like to live there. A sand flea is just a regular flea that lives in sand.

Some people believe that feeding their pets garlic will keep fleas away. Since garlic has such a strong smell, they think that the fleas will try to get away from the odor. It would be great if it worked, but there's no scientific proof that it does work. If it did, all we would have to do is feed Fido some garlic bread with his pesto, and presto! No more fleas!

FLEA Facts

- A flea that lives 6 to 8 weeks can lay 2,000 eggs in her life span.

- Americans spend more than $1 billion each year fighting fleas.

- Vibrations can make a flea hatch.

- A flea's life cycle can stretch from 2 weeks to 2 years.

- Most fleas attack mammals, such as humans, dogs, and cats. Some attack birds.

- In 30 days, 10 female fleas can multiply to more than 250,000 fleas in various stages.

- There are more than 250 species of fleas in North America.

ZOOM CAM

Do You Want to Know More?

Log on to these Web sites to learn more about fleas:

- http://www.greensmiths.com/fleas.htm
- http://www.ag.ohio-state.edu/~ohioline/hyg-fact/2000/2081.html
- http://www.cdfa.ca.gov/agfacts/pesticides/fleas.html
- http://www.colostate.edu/Depts/IPM/natparks/fleas.html
- http://www.orkin.com/fleas/fleas.html
- http://www.ianr.unl.edu/ianr/lanco/enviro/pest/factsheets/fleas.html
- http://trivia.lsds.com/Animals/Fleas.html
- http://www.biohaven.com/fleas.htm

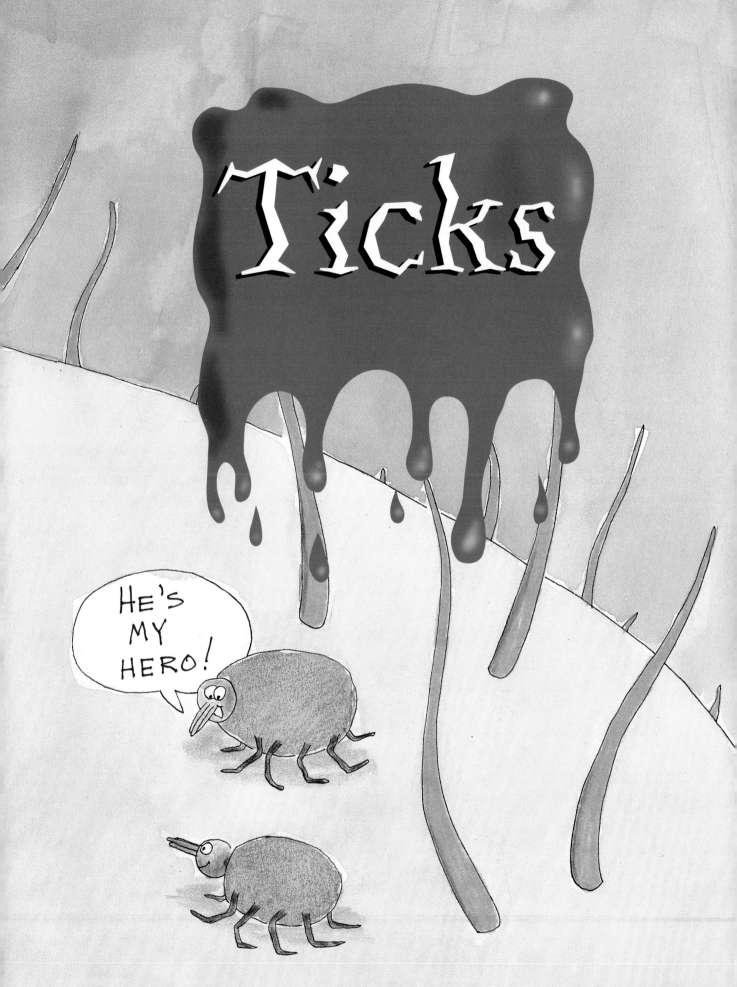

Types of TICKS

There are more than 800 species of ticks, and they are divided into two basic families: hard ticks and soft ticks. Unlike mosquitoes and fleas, ticks are not insects. They are more closely related to spiders. A tick digs its mouth parts into the flesh of its victim and sucks the blood. As it continues to feed, the tick's body starts to swell until the tick has become many times its normal size. Ticks especially like to bite around the victim's head, neck, and ears.

DISEASE

Ticks are the champs when it comes to carrying diseases. You might say:

I THINK I'VE GOT SPOTTED FEVER.

"When it comes to making people sick, Nothing's better than a tick."

Ticks transmit lots of different bacteria and viruses. You may have heard of Lyme disease and Rocky Mountain Spotted Fever. Ticks spread both of those diseases.

Ticks undergo a number of changes during their lifetimes. Like the other creatures we've seen, ticks start out as eggs. One of the amazing things about female ticks is the number of eggs they lay. Usually it's thousands at a time!

Life Stages of a TICK

When the tick emerges from its egg, it begins its life as a larva. Unlike some of the other bloodsucking creatures we've seen, tick larvae are not wormlike. Instead, they have six legs. This is really weird, because in all future stages of a tick's life, the tick has eight legs, like a spider! After a brief stage as a nymph, the tick becomes a full-grown adult.

How Do They EAT?

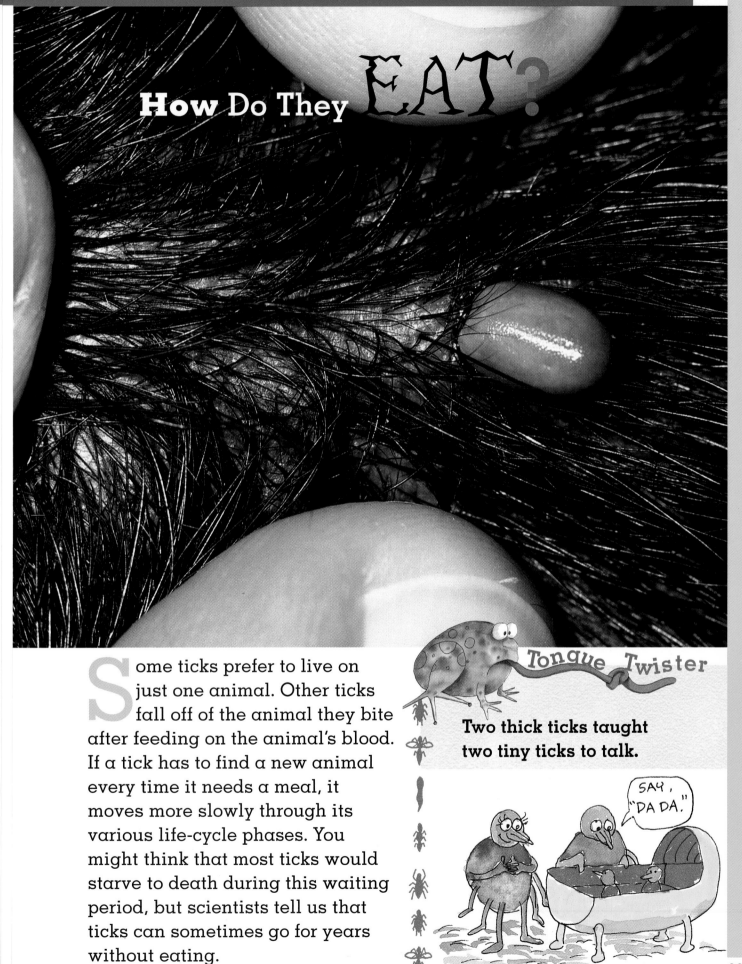

Some ticks prefer to live on just one animal. Other ticks fall off of the animal they bite after feeding on the animal's blood. If a tick has to find a new animal every time it needs a meal, it moves more slowly through its various life-cycle phases. You might think that most ticks would starve to death during this waiting period, but scientists tell us that ticks can sometimes go for years without eating.

Tongue Twister

Two thick ticks taught two tiny ticks to talk.

SAY, "DA DA."

Lots of Lice

There are about 200 species of sucking lice, but only 3 species attack humans. The species that people know best is called "head lice." Head lice live in your hair and suck your blood. Then they attach their eggs to your hair and let the heat from your body keep the eggs nice and warm until they're ready to hatch. Pretty soon, the whole lice family is having a party on your head!

Backyard Bloodsuckers Bulletin

Head lice can crawl fast, but they can't jump or hop. They can't fly either. They don't have wings.

An itchy scalp might be a sign that lice have made a home on your head. As the louse digs into a human scalp, chemicals in its saliva (spit) irritate the skin and cause itching. It can sometimes even cause a rash.

How Do They SPREAD?

Just because someone has head lice doesn't mean that person is dirty. In fact, anybody can get head lice. Lice get passed from person to person by direct contact. That means if you share a comb, a brush, or even a hat, the lice could move from another person's head to yours, even if your head is perfectly clean.

WOO HOO!

YiPEE!

Backyard Bloodsuckers Bulletin

Health organizations estimate that there are 12 million cases of head lice each year.

How Do I REMOVE Them?

One of the best ways to remove the nits (eggs) is to comb the hair with a fine-toothed comb. As the comb is pulled through the hair, the teeth of the comb will break the glue that sticks the nit to the hair shaft.

Some people use strong chemicals to kill nits, but others think this is a bad idea since the chemicals have to be placed on the heads of children.

The normal life span of a louse is about 30 days. The female louse lays about 150 eggs in a month. It's easy to mistake other things in the hair for nits. Sometimes dandruff and dead skin can look a lot like nits. But if a person shampoos his or her hair and there's still some little whitish-tan specks sticking to the hair shaft, it's a good bet that that person has head lice.

Backyard Bloodsuckers Bulletin

In World War I, the soldiers nicknamed head lice "galloping dandruff."

GIDDY UP!

Life Stages of a LOUSE

It takes about 10 days for the nits to hatch. When they do, a nymph emerges. Nymphs are hungry little critters. As soon as they emerge from the egg, they're ready to eat. They generally need to feed on some blood about every 3 to 6 hours. Over the next 2 weeks, the nymph goes through three stages before it becomes an adult and is ready to reproduce.

Most of the time, lice are found where humans have hair. Body lice, however, actually live in the seams of clothing and bedding. They come out to eat, then go back into the clothing. If your clothes are washed regularly, you probably don't have to worry too much about body lice.

IF YOU'RE IN THERE, COME OUT WITH YOUR HANDS UP.

Backyard Bloodsuckers Bulletin

Lice have strong claws that they use to hold onto hair shafts and clothing fabric.

Other Kinds of LICE

Some lice live only on animals. For instance, the sheep louse lives only on (you guessed it!) sheep. The sheep louse is very small and lays only 3 eggs every 5 days. The sheep body louse is different from the kind of louse that sucks human blood. In fact, sheep body lice don't suck blood at all. They just live on the small stuff they can scrounge off the skin of the sheep.

EWE?

EEEYEWW...

YUM!

Tongue Twister

Eleven little lazy lice licked licorice lollipops.

Leads on Lice

- Head lice live in your hair.

- The eggs of head lice are called nits.

- Anyone can get head lice.

- Once lice hatch, they need to feed on blood about every 3 to 6 hours.

- Lice use their strong claws to hold onto hair shafts.

- Some lice live on humans; some live on animals.

ZOOM CAM

Do You Want to Know More?

Log on to these Web sites to learn more about lice:

- http://www.newton.dep.anl.gov/natbltn/200-299/nb292.htm

- http://www.headlice.org/

- http://www.jcu.edu.au/school/phtm/PHTM/hlice/hlinfo1.htm

- http://www.nandotimes.com/newsroom/ntn/health/041896/health12_1117.html

- http://www.netmedicine.com/pt/PTINFO/pedi.htm

- http://www.drgreene.com/970213.html

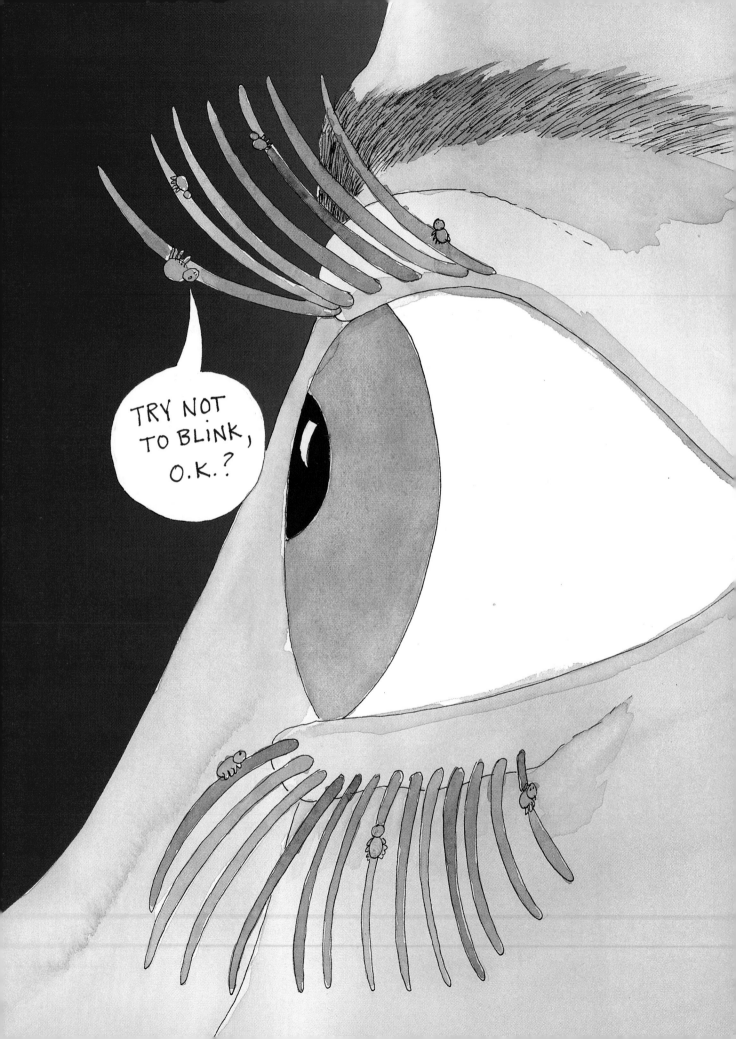

Mites and Chiggers

MITES

Technically, mites aren't bloodsuckers. They're more like "dissolved-tissue suckers." Why? Because as they dig into human or animal skin, they inject saliva (spit), which contains chemicals that dissolve the tissues of the victim. Then they suck up the juicy dissolved tissue for a tasty meal.

Like many other parasites in this book, mites go through four stages of life: egg, larva, nymph, and adult.

NOW I'M REALLY SICK!

Although most mites are found on the surface of the skin, some live inside the bodies of animals.

Mites are not insects. They're more like ticks and spiders. In fact, when mites hatch from their eggs, they have six legs, just like tick larvae. Later, they develop two more legs, for a total of eight.

I AM NOT AN INSECT!

SCABIES Mites

One particularly irritating mite is the scabies mite. The female scabies mite chews into the skin of its host and feeds on the body fluids. After she feeds, she lays about 3 eggs in the little tunnel she dug. In 3 or 4 days the larvae emerge from the eggs. Soon the larvae molt and become nymphs.

When the nymphs start burrowing into the skin and feeding, they can cause an itchy rash. That's generally the first sign that scabies mites have found a home on somebody's body. After the nymphs have been feeding a while, they molt again and become adults. The entire life cycle of the mite normally takes about 2 weeks.

Backyard Bloodsuckers Bulletin

When a creature molts, it sheds its outer layer of skin or shell so it can grow. Lots of creatures molt, even snakes and crabs!

HMM... MAYBE I'D BETTER MOLT.

A scabies mite is "host-specific." That means that it doesn't move from one kind of creature to another during its life cycle. It may "hitch a ride" for a while and cause some itching, but it won't raise its family there.

Like many other backyard bloodsuckers, scabies mites need to eat every few hours. In fact, a scabies mite will die if it is separated from its food source for more than 24 hours.

Microscopic MITES

Although many mites can be seen easily, some are so tiny you need a microscope to see them. Here are two examples:

House Dust Mites

These little guys live in your carpet and mattresses at home and can cause you some big problems if you have allergies. About half of the homes in the United States are infested with dust mites. In the average mattress, there could be 1 million to 2 million dust mites. They're very tiny critters that live off of dead skin cells and other yummy stuff. Unfortunately, their feces can cause asthma and allergic reactions in many people. Steam-cleaning carpets can help keep their numbers down.

Follicle Mites

You're not going to like this next sentence. At this very moment, there is an excellent chance that you have follicle mites crawling all over your eyelashes. That's right. Most people have follicle mites living on the hairs of their eyelids or on the glands near the surface. Even though you can't see them, they're there. But don't worry. They don't bite and they won't bother you.

Bloodsucking Flies

Types of Bloodsucking FLIES

There are lots of bloodsucking flies that are real pests to humans and animals. Here are just a few:

Stable Flies

As you can guess by its name, the stable fly can be found in stables, barns, and other places where animals are sheltered. But they can also be found in open areas

such as pastures. Unlike some of the other bloodsuckers we've seen, it's not only the female stable fly that sucks blood. The males do too. Their bites can be very painful.

Females must have a blood meal before they can produce eggs. They like to lay their eggs in some rotting vegetation mixed with manure. Within a few days, the eggs hatch into larvae. The larvae grow through several larval stages until they become pupae. In a week or two, they become adults. The entire life cycle takes about 2 to 5 weeks.

Stable flies don't actually live on animals and people. They just visit them when they get hungry. Stable flies are a real bother to cattle. Dairy farmers and ranchers work hard to keep the stables and barns clean so stable flies don't have places to breed.

Backyard Bloodsuckers
Bulletin

A female stable fly may lay as many as 400 eggs during her short lifetime.

Horn Flies

Unlike stable flies, horn flies do not bite people, but they love to bite horses and cows! You can tell how irritating these little pests are by their scientific name: Haematobia irritans.

When it's hot outside, you can sometimes see horn flies on the backs, shoulders, and undersides of cattle. That's where they live . . . in the hair of the animal. The really bad news is that both male and female horn flies bite and they can feed as many as 40 times each day. Ouch!

Backyard Bloodsuckers Bulletin

It's not unusual to see 500 or more horn flies on a single cow or horse infested with horn flies.

After the females feed, they leave the animal and lay their eggs in fresh manure. The eggs hatch into larvae that grow into pupae in 1 or 2 weeks. The pupae take another week or two to grow into adults and the cycle begins again.

Face Flies

Can you imagine your face covered with biting flies? Blaaah! Disgusting! In the southern United States there's a fly called the face fly that likes to feed on blood and other fluids around the eyes and noses of cattle.

You can imagine how irritating this is to cattle. Often, when there are lots of face flies around, cattle will crowd together to try to protect themselves.

WE'RE NOT BOTHERING YOU, ARE WE?

(HEE HEE)

Like the horn fly, the face fly prefers to stay outside, although it will seek shelter indoors during winter months. Also like the horn fly, the face fly goes through four stages: egg, larva, pupa, and adult. The entire life cycle of the face fly takes only about 3 weeks to complete.

Tongue Twister

Fifty-five face flies flew fast.

FINISH

I WIN!

Tsetse (pronounced "SEAT see") Flies

In some parts of the world, tsetse flies kill tens of thousands of people each year. The good news is you're not likely to see any tsetse flies unless you visit the tropical regions of Africa.

Tsetse flies live only on blood and can transmit a disease called "sleeping sickness." It's a very serious disease, but it can be treated if the person who is bitten can get to a doctor quickly.

Female tsetse flies do not lay eggs, but instead give birth to a single full-grown larva. The larva immediately turns into a pupa. A short time later, it becomes a full-grown adult.

One of the ways scientists are controlling the population of tsetse flies is by exposing male tsetse flies to radiation. This makes the males unable to reproduce. Since tsetse flies usually only mate once before they die, many female tsetse flies mate with these males and then die without producing any offspring. Scientists have also used traps to catch tsetse flies, but these haven't been as effective. In addition to making humans sick, tsetse flies also transmit diseases to cattle.

Insect MUSEUMS

Are you interested in seeing some critters up close? If so, you might try to visit some of these insect museums:

If you're in the Philadelphia area, you may want to visit the Philadelphia Insectarium. It has a cockroach kitchen, a live termite tunnel, and other cool exhibits. Call (215) 338-3000 for more information.

The Bohart Museum is located on the campus of the University of California in Davis, CA. The museum has an arthropod petting zoo as well as their "Oh My!" collection. Call (530) 752-0493 for more information.

The Museum of Biological Diversity on the campus of Ohio State University has more than 3.5 million specimens. They do allow visitors, but it's best to call before you visit. Phone: (614) 292-2730.

The University of Wyoming in Laramie, WY, has an Insect Museum that houses the world's largest collection (60,000 specimens) of a specific parasitic wasp that lives in Costa Rica. They also have a live insect zoo, insect hand stamps, insect models, and lots more. Call the University of Wyoming for more information. Phone: (307) 766-1121.

If you live in the central United States, you might want to visit the Entomology Museum on the campus of the University of Missouri in Columbia, MO. This museum has been around for more than 100 years and currently holds almost 6 million specimens of insects, arachnids, and fossils. The collection can be seen, but be sure you call first. Sometimes the scientists are outside tracking down new bugs for their collection. Phone: (573) 882-2410.

If you're in Canada, the Newfoundland Insectarium is a great place to see insects and arachnids up close. This place has lots of giant things—giant water bugs, giant beetles, and giant scorpions. Great fun! Phone: (709) 635-4545.

Buckets of Info on Bloodsucking Flies

- Both male and female stable flies suck blood.

- Horn flies can feed as many as 40 times each day.

- Face flies feed on the fluids around the faces of cattle.

- Tsetse flies are found in Africa.

- Tsetse flies do not lay eggs.

Do You Want to Know More?

Log on to these Web sites to learn more about biting flies:

- http://biodidac.bio.uottawa.ca/Thumbnails/DIPT003B-GIF.htm
- http://www.parasitology.org/Imgbank/Arthrimg.htm
- http://res.agr.ca/ecorc/apss/fly/stable.htm
- http://res.agr.ca/ecorc/apss/fly/horn.htm
- http://www.biosci.ohio-state.edu/~parasite/trypanosoma.html
- http://res.agr.ca/ecorc/apss/fly/face.htm
- http://www.fao.org/NEWS/1998/980505-e.htm
- http://www2.sel.barc.usda.gov/Diptera/dips/simuli.htm

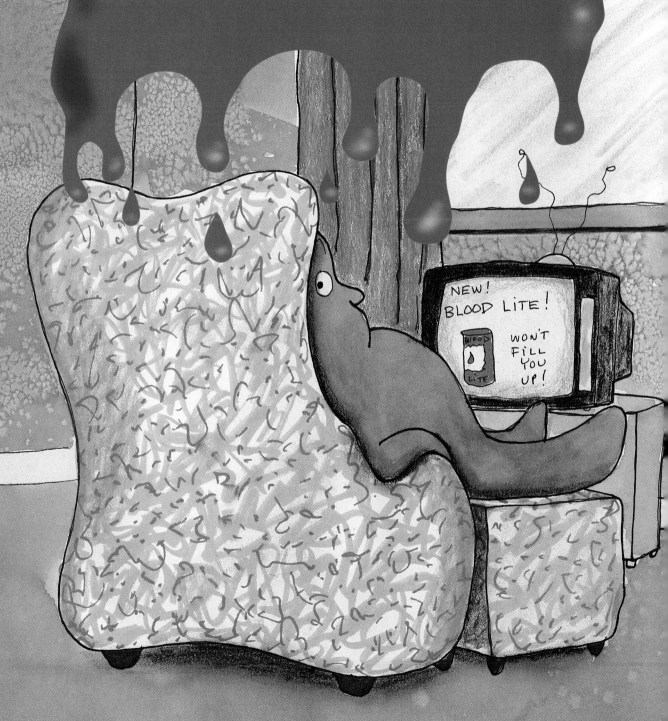

Loads of LEECHES

Unlike some of the other bloodsuckers we've seen, leeches are not insects. And they're not related to ticks and spiders. Leeches are actually worms. And even though leeches are hungry bloodsuckers, they can be very helpful to humans. Here's how: When a leech bites a person, it injects fluids that open the person's blood vessels and keep the blood flowing. This makes the job of sucking blood easier for the leech. These fluids are so effective that blood from a leech bite will continue to flow as long as 2 days after the leech has bitten the person (although 6 hours is the average). Knowing this, doctors have used leeches to help people whose ear, finger, or other body part has been cut off and reattached. Doctors attach leeches to the injured area and let the leeches feed. As they feed, the leeches keep the blood flowing to the area. This makes it possible for the body part to heal and become healthy again.

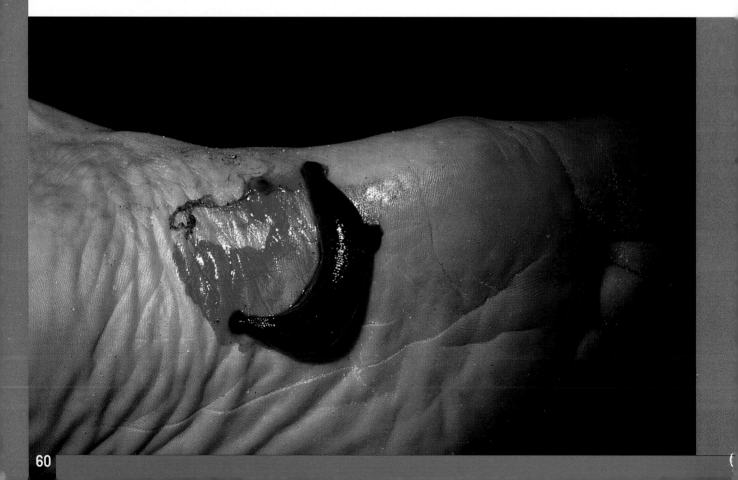

Medical Uses of LEECHES

Doctors also use leeches to remove "pools" of blood that are not flowing well under the skin of humans. Leeches have become so popular for medical uses that one company in England ships more than 20,000 leeches a year to doctors and hospitals.

Long ago, doctors believed that people could be cured of many different illnesses if some of their blood was removed. It sounds crazy to us today, but they didn't know all we know about how the human body works. When it came time to remove the blood, doctors would sometimes make a cut in the person's arm and let the blood drain. Other times, the doctor would stick hungry leeches on the person's arm and let the leeches feed until the leeches were nice and fat.

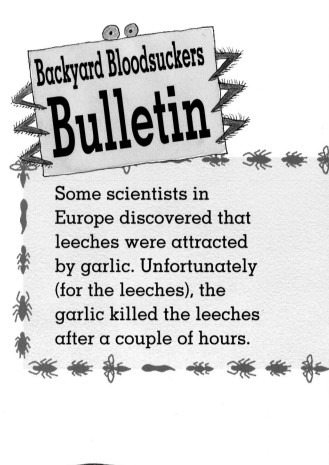

Backyard Bloodsuckers Bulletin

Some scientists in Europe discovered that leeches were attracted by garlic. Unfortunately (for the leeches), the garlic killed the leeches after a couple of hours.

RELAX. THIS WON'T HURT...

MUCH.

Leech MUSEUM

Would you like to spend a little "quality time" with some real live leeches? In Illinois, there's a lady who spends time with live leeches every day. Her name is Barbara Mason, and she is the curator of the Pearson Museum.

The Pearson Museum is part of the Southern Illinois School of Medicine in Springfield, Illinois, and it contains some pretty strange stuff. In the "Bloodsuckers" department, there are plenty of leeches, and Ms. Mason will be happy to show you her live specimens. There are also other medical exhibits that deal with blood-letting. Blood-letting was the practice of draining the blood from people who were ill or bothered by physical ailments. People used to believe that if they drained blood from sick people, they could make the sick people feel better. Pretty weird, huh?

While you're at the museum, don't forget to ask Ms. Mason to show you the mummified human hand too!

You can contact Ms. Mason at the Pearson Museum by phoning (217) 785-2128. The museum is located at 801 North Rutlidge Street in Springfield, Illinois.

THOSE ARE SOME REALLY WEIRD-LOOKING CREATURES...

What Do They EAT?

How much do you weigh? Imagine eating five times your weight in food at one meal! That's what leeches do. It's true! A typical leech can eat five times its body weight in blood at one "meal." When leeches are in the water, their bodies ripple up and down like a wave. When they are out of the water, they use their suckers (one on each end of their bodies) to grab hold and pull themselves forward.

One of the reasons why people generally don't feel a leech bite them is because the leech's saliva (spit) contains a chemical that deadens the skin where it's biting. Generally, it's only after the leech has been feeding a while that the victim realizes that he or she has become the leech's dinner.

How Do I REMOVE It?

As repulsive as a leech is, it's probably not a good idea to tear it off of your skin if you find one on you. That's because the leech has strong "grabbers" in its mouth, and you might leave the "grabbers" in your skin if you rip the leech off too hard. The mouth parts could then become infected. It's better to put some salt or something hot (but not too hot) on the leech to make it let go.

And be prepared for some bleeding if you remove a leech. Remember, one of the things it does best is keep the blood flowing. If you remove a leech, your blood will probably flow for a short while.

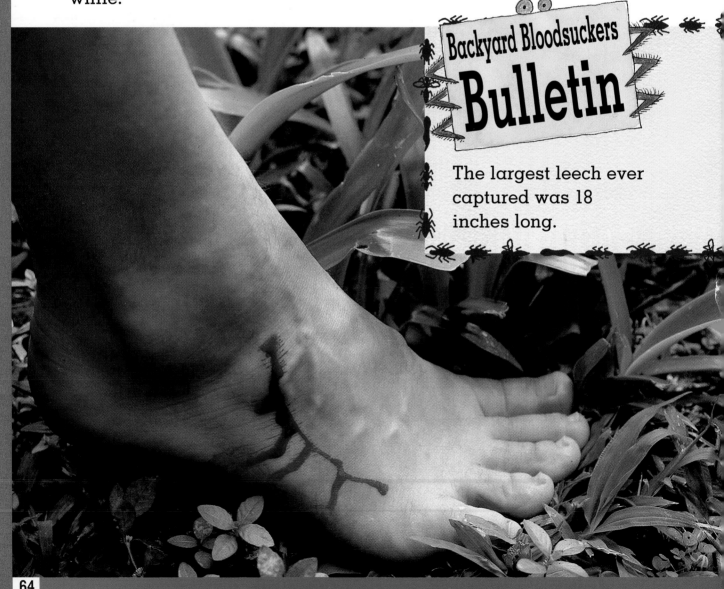

Backyard Bloodsuckers Bulletin

The largest leech ever captured was 18 inches long.

Where Do They LIVE?

Leeches are most often found in ponds, lakes, and rivers, but about 20 percent of the leech species live in the sea, where they attach themselves to fish and feed off of the fish's blood.

Even though we think of leeches as bloodsucking creatures, not all leeches suck blood. Many leeches are predators and live by eating earthworms and other small creatures.

In some parts of the United States, people who like to fish buy leeches as bait.

What Kind of ANIMAL Is a Leech?

Do you know what some leeches and frogs have in common? They're amphibious! That means they can live on land or on water. Even though some leeches are amphibious, that doesn't mean they're amphibians. Amphibians are animals, such as frogs, salamanders, and newts. Amphibians have backbones. Leeches are a kind of weird worm called annelids . . . they don't have backbones.

Backyard Bloodsuckers Bulletin

Leeches aren't just warm-weather creatures. Some leeches have been found in waters near the Antarctic!

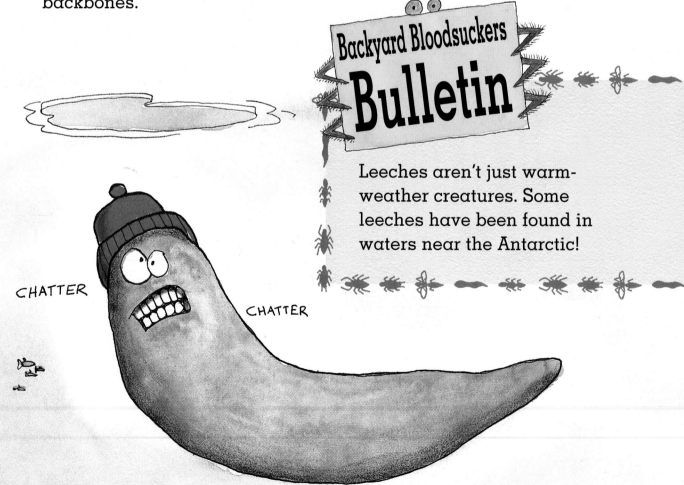

CHATTER

CHATTER

Lots of Info on LEECHES

- Leeches are worms.

- Leeches can be helpful to humans.

- A leech can eat five times its weight in blood.

- A chemical in a leech's saliva deadens human skin.

- After a leech is removed, blood will continue to flow for a while.

Do You Want to Know More?

Log on to these Web sites to learn more about leeches:

- http://www.gene.com/AE/LC/SS/leechlove.html

- http://www.fluvarium.nf.net/invert.htm

- http://www.uib.no/isf/surprise.htm

- http://www.leechesusa.com/case1.htm

- http://www2.nando.net/newsroom/ntn/health/092398/health27_12278_body.html

- http://www.zetatalk.com/health/theall1a.htm

- http://www.eng.us.uu.net/staff/jeff/leeches.html

- http://www.nj.com/yucky/worm/reporter/leech.html

[NO FRIEND OF FISH]

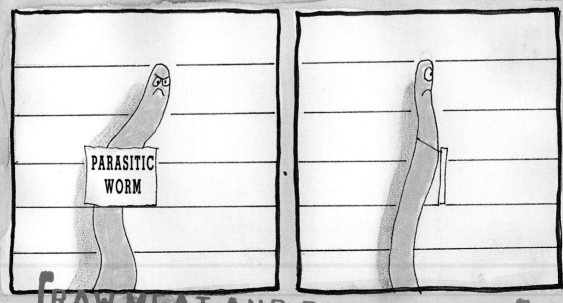

[RAW MEAT AND DIRTY HANDS
ARE HIS HANGOUTS]

Other Bloodsuckers

AMOEBA

[DIRTY WATER DUDE]

Parasitic WORMS

Parasites are creatures that live off of the bodies of other creatures. So far, the creatures we've seen all live on the outside of humans and animals. They only bite and dig into our skin when they want to eat. But some creatures actually live inside of humans and animals. As you might imagine, these animals are very small. They include tapeworms and pinworms. These little pests can really upset your stomach, and millions of people around the world get sick every year because of them. The best way to avoid these critters is to wash your hands regularly and make sure your food is cooked well.

Log on to these Web sites to learn more about these creatures:

- http://www.biosci.ohio-state.edu/~parasite/images.html
- http://www.nj.com/yucky/worm/reporter/tape.html
- http://martin.parasitology.mcgill.ca/JIMSPAGE/stongylioides.htm
- http://martin.parasitology.mcgill.ca/JIMSPAGE/ENTEROBI.HTM
- http://martin.parasitology.mcgill.ca/JIMSPAGE/TRICHINE.HTM
- http://martin.parasitology.mcgill.ca/JIMSPAGE/ECHINO.HTM
- http://martin.parasitology.mcgill.ca/JIMSPAGE/vamp.htm

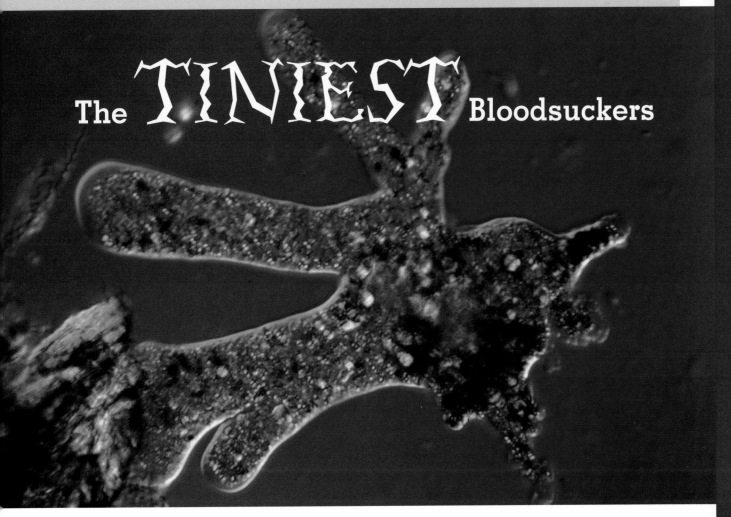

The TINIEST Bloodsuckers

Amoebas and protozoans are very tiny, microscopic creatures that can cause a lot of trouble. They can give people dysentery and other nasty diseases. In poorer countries where the people don't have clean drinking water, they may drink water that has these parasites in it. This can make the people very sick. Sometimes, even in the United States, after a flood or a hurricane, there's not enough clean drinking water in certain places. When this happens, people can avoid amoebas and protozoans by drinking bottled water. Since our bodies are mostly water, it's important that the water we drink is clean and healthy.

Log on to these Web sites to learn more about amoebas and protozoans:

- http://martin.parasitology.mcgill.ca/JIMSPAGE/amoeba.HTM
- http://martin.parasitology.mcgill.ca/JIMSPAGE/GIARDIA.HTM

LAMPREYS

If you were a fish, you would not like to see a lamprey headed your way. Lampreys have a large mouth that's like a vacuum cleaner. When a fish swims by, the lamprey attaches itself to the fish with its big vacuum-cleaner mouth.

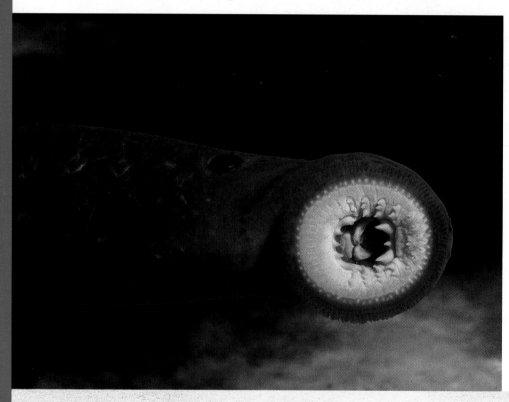

Then, the lamprey uses its rough, sharp tongue to cut a hole in the side of the fish (ouch!) and begins sucking out the fish's fluids. Yuck! A single lamprey can kill many fish this way.

NOW THAT IS VERY, VERY CREEPY!

Log on to these Web sites to learn more about lampreys:

- http://www.fws.gov/r3pao/marqette/etc/mouth.html
- http://nativefish.interspeed.net/Articles/Lampreys.htm
- http://www.cen.uiuc.edu/~n-chazin/lamprey.html

Studying INSECTS

Many insects eat smaller insects. Those insects in turn are eaten by birds, fish, and other creatures. Then larger animals eat the birds and fish. This cycle of larger creatures eating smaller creatures is called "the food chain." Even though most of the creatures in this book are pesky to humans, they are very important in the food chain.

If there are too many pests in an area, humans and their pets can become sick. If there are not enough pests for other animals to eat, those animals might starve. Scientists are working hard to help nature maintain its "pest" balance. If you're interested in this kind of work, you may think about becoming an entomologist. An entomologist studies insects. Some entomologists are interested in finding safe ways to reduce the number of insects. Others study the ways insects reproduce and spread disease. To learn more, ask the media specialist at your library for information about the work that entomologists do.

Your school library or public library has some other great books about insects, arachnids, and other parasites. If you'd like to visit some interesting Web sites, try these:

- http://www.pestweb.com/insects/index.html
This site has information about insects and other creatures. It's a good place to start.

- http://www.ent.iastate.edu/list/ k-12_educator_resources.html
This site has great info and ways to contact insect experts.

- http://www.eatbug.com/
Hungry? There are more than 1,400 insects that you can eat!

- http://www-museum.unl.edu/ asp/photo.html
This is the place to visit if you want to see pictures of disgusting critters.

- http://www.bos.nl/homes/bijlmakers/ento/begin.html
This is a good site to visit to learn basic information about insects.

- http://falcon.jmu.edu/~ramseyil/lifescience.htm
Another great "basic" site with tons of information.

GLOSSARY

Amoebas Microscopic creatures that live inside animals and may cause disease.

Arachnids Creatures, such as ticks and spiders, who have eight legs.

Arthropods Creatures whose skeletons are on the outside of their bodies and who have legs with joints.

Carbon Dioxide The gas that humans and animals breathe out of their lungs.

Cocoon A tube or container spun by a pupa; used as protection for continued growth.

Dysentery A disease caused by amoebas.

Entomologist A scientist that studies insects.

Feces Animal waste; also known as manure or droppings.

Follicle A shaft of hair.

Insects Creatures, such as mosquitoes, flies, and fleas, who have six legs.

Larva The stage of development that follows the egg stage.

Lyme disease A disease spread by ticks, characterized by fever, joint pain, and red, circular spots on the skin.

Malaria One of the diseases transmitted by mosquitoes.

Molt Process during which an animal sheds its outer layer of skin or skeleton so it can grow.

Nits Another word for lice eggs.

Nymph A young insect or other small creature that has not fully developed into an adult but looks very much like the adult in shape.

Parasite A creature that lives off of another creature.

Pesticides Chemicals designed to kill pests.

Plague A diseases spread by fleas in the fourteenth century; also called the "Black Death."

Plasma A substance in human blood that contains the proteins some bloodsuckers need to reproduce.

Platelets The substance in blood that stops bleeding and helps blood clot.

Predator An animal that eats other animals.

Pupa The stage of development that follows the larva stage.

Red blood cells Blood cells that carry oxygen to the rest of the body.

Saliva Another word for "spit."

Trumpets Breathing tubes used by mosquito pupae.

White blood cells Blood cells that fight infection.

Yellow fever A disease transmitted by mosquitoes.

Photocopy these "backyard bloodsucker" silhouettes, cut out each one, and project the image on the overhead projector in your classroom as you discuss each creature.

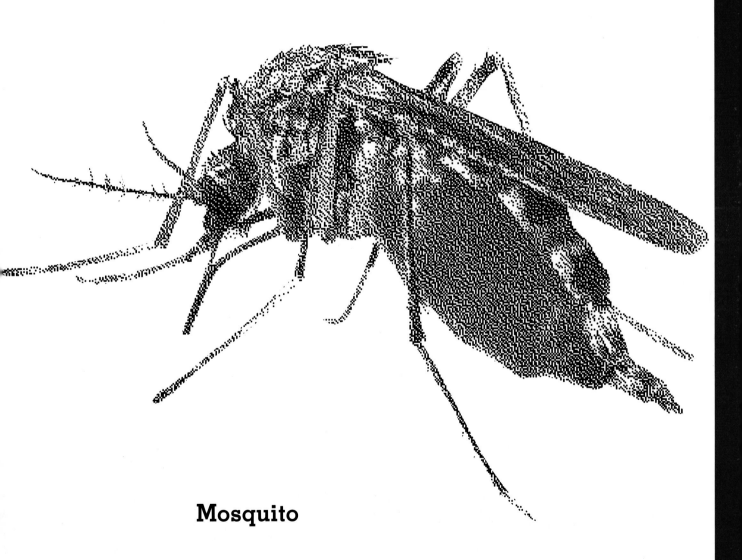

Mosquito

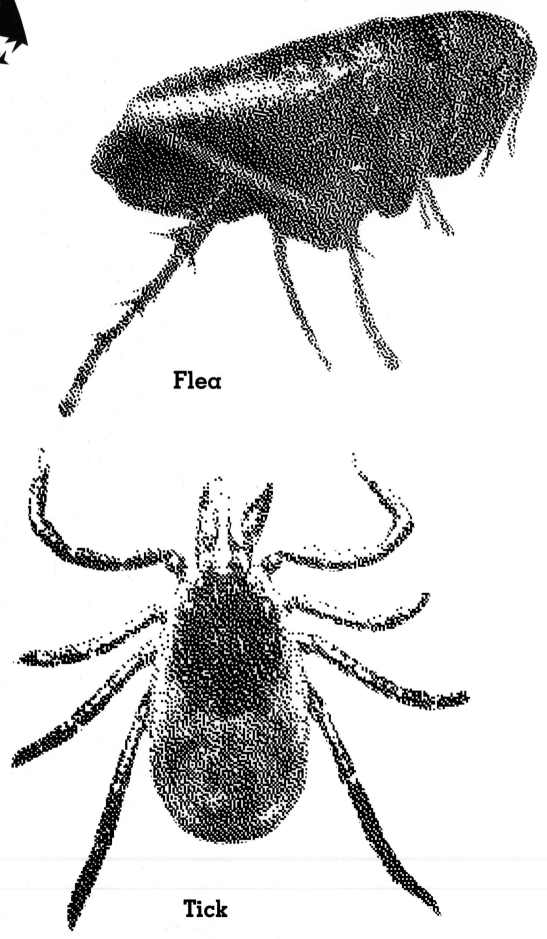

Flea

Tick

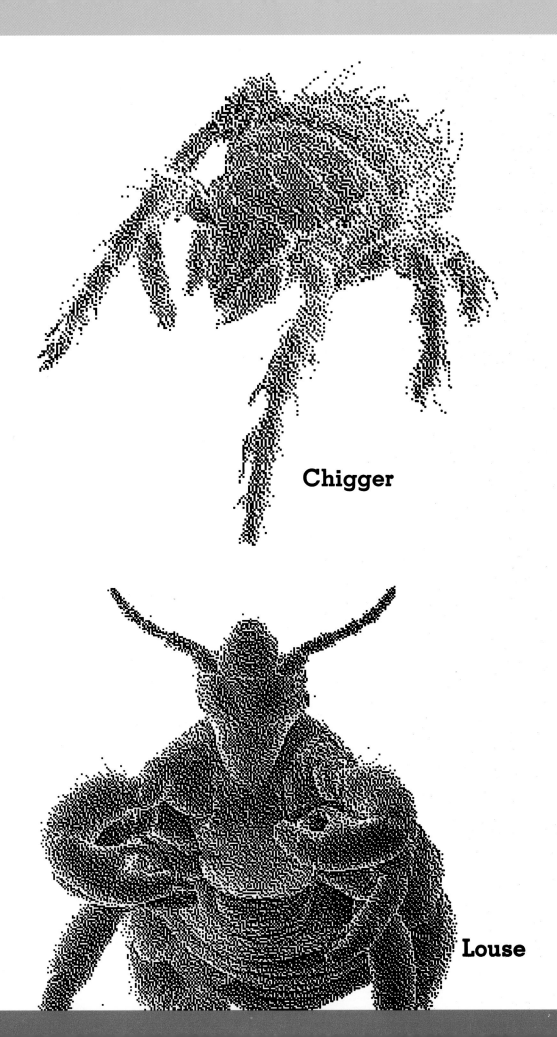

Chigger

Louse

Fly

Leech

FINAL NOTE

You don't have to go on a long field trip to see interesting sights.
You can find lots of interesting creatures in your own backyard or
in a nearby park. The next time you're outside, sit on the ground,
move the grass around a little, and see if you can find any little
critters moving around. Check near the bottoms of nearby trees for
other creatures too. Then look on the underside of leaves and
flowers. Roll a rock over and look underneath. You'll be amazed by
all the life you'll find.

Don't just watch the world on television. Get out and explore! If
you're lucky, you may find some backyard bloodsuckers. Good luck!

Other Science Books by Mike Artell
The Earth & Me (with Pam Schiller)
Starry Skies
Weather Whys

Some Nonscience Books by Mike Artell
Awesome Alphabets
Classroom Cartooning
Parties Kids Love

Would you like to contact Mike? Send him an e-mail:

mikeartell@aol.com